Spotlight on Climate Change

Arctic Ice Loss

Abbe L. Starr

Lerner Publications ◆ Minneapolis

Lerner Publications Company
An imprint of Lerner Publishing Group, Inc.
241 First Avenue North
Minneapolis, MN 55401 USA

For reading levels and more information, look up this title at www.lernerbooks.com.

Main body text set in Adrianna Regular.
Typeface provided by Chank.

Editor: Brianna Kaiser

Library of Congress Cataloging-in-Publication Data

Names: Starr, Abbe L., author.
Title: Arctic ice loss / Abbe L. Starr.
Description: Minneapolis : Lerner Publications, [2023] | Series: Searchlight books - spotlight on climate change | Includes bibliographical references and index. | Audience: Ages 8–11 | Audience: Grades 2–3 | Summary: "Discover the ways Arctic ice loss is affecting Earth's animals and sea levels. With eye-catching photos and fascinating facts, this book takes a thorough look at Arctic ice loss"— Provided by publisher.
Identifiers: LCCN 2021051340 (print) | LCCN 2021051341 (ebook) | ISBN 9781728457925 (library binding) | ISBN 9781728463896 (paperback) | ISBN 9781728461878 (ebook)
Subjects: LCSH: Climatic changes—Arctic regions—Juvenile literature. | Sea ice—Climatic factors—Arctic regions—Juvenile literature. | Habitat conservation—Arctic regions—Juvenile literature. | Sea level—Climatic factors—Arctic regions—Juvenile literature.
Classification: LCC QC903.2.A68 S73 2023 (print) | LCC QC903.2.A68 (ebook) | DDC 551.34/3091632—dc23/eng/20211204

LC record available at https://lccn.loc.gov/2021051340
LC ebook record available at https://lccn.loc.gov/2021051341

Manufactured in the United States of America
1-50820-50159-2/14/2022

Table of Contents

Chapter 1

WHAT IS ARCTIC SEA ICE?

The Arctic Ocean covers the most northern part of Earth. It is the smallest, shallowest, and coldest of the five oceans. Arctic sea ice is frozen ocean water that forms, grows, and melts in the ocean. Every year ice in the Arctic goes through a growth and melting cycle. It grows to its largest extent around March and melts to its lowest extent around September.

The Arctic is one of the environments most at risk to climate change. Earth's climate can change due to natural factors like volcanoes, weather patterns, and the position of Earth to the sun. But scientists agree that human activity is the main factor causing Earth's climate to change. As Earth's climate changes, so does the Arctic.

Austfonna, located in Norway's Svalbard archipelago, is one of the largest ice caps in northern Europe.

Measuring Ice

Researchers from the National Snow and Ice Data Center measure Arctic ice because it tells them about climate change. They study how far the ice extends and  how much ice grows in a certain area. They also measure how thick the ice is above and below the surface. Younger ice is thinner and more likely to melt in the summer months than older, thicker ice.

Many Alaskans use unghaqs, ice testing sticks, when they walk and hunt on the ice so they can test the ice's thickness and move safely.

Polar researcher Roman Gouzenko drills into Arctic ice.

Scientists measure ice in multiple ways. They collect data recorded from satellites. The data has been recorded since 1978. Satellites measure how much ice covers the Arctic in all seasons. Newer satellites give estimates for ice thickness, but there is not yet long-term data.

For a closer look, field researchers drill holes deep into the ice. The oldest ice can be up to 15 feet (4.6 m) deep. They also pull sleds with sensors. The sensors send electromagnetic pulses, or short bursts of energy, into the ice to estimate the thickness of the ice below. Buoys that float on the sea ice or in Arctic waters also collect data.

An iceberg
in Greenland

For a deeper look, submarines dive below the ice. They use a device called an upward-looking sonar to measure the thickness of the ice.

Scientists have discovered that less ice currently survives in the Arctic than when they began their research in 1978. Ice that does last through the summer months is thinner and more fragile than it used to be. Because the ice is melting faster in the summer than it is growing in the winter, the overall ice cover has decreased year-round in the Arctic regions.

Shari Fox

Shari Fox is a research scientist at the National Snow and Ice Data Center. She studies changes in the Arctic environment and its weather conditions. Fox investigates Arctic rain on snow and how it affects wildlife and communities. She also gathers research with Inuit community members. Together, they search for ways to secure water, energy, and food. Fox studies the future of Inuit regions and how they will adapt to climate change.

Chapter 2

WHY IS ARCTIC ICE IMPORTANT?

Arctic sea ice is mostly surrounded by land. The ice floats but usually stays in the freezing cold water. Separate patches of floating ice, called floes, bump and crash into one another as they are pushed around by waves, wind, and ocean currents. This causes the ice to pile up and create small mountains with sharp ridges. This also makes thick Arctic ice.

This Arctic ice has a very important job. Acting like a giant air conditioner, it keeps Arctic water and air temperatures cool.

Arctic ice also reflects sunlight. The ice is bright white or sometimes bright gray. Sunlight hits the ice's bright surface and is reflected back into space. When the ice melts in the summer months, sunlight is absorbed by the ocean. This causes the oceans to heat up and increases Arctic temperatures.

A harbor seal rests on ice in Alaska.

Sunlight brings both heat and energy to Earth. The reflection from the Arctic ice keeps the heat and energy in balance, making certain that the power of the sun isn't too strong for Earth to absorb.

Measurements show that sea ice is becoming thinner and covers less area. Losing sea ice makes Earth warm quicker and could make global climate change happen faster.

Ice Albedo

Scientists study the albedo of Earth's surfaces. That means they measure how much energy from the sun is reflected by a surface. Sea ice has one of the highest albedos of Earth's surfaces. It can reflect 50 to 70 percent of energy. Since sea ice reflects more solar energy than it absorbs, it keeps Earth's surface cooler.

Arctic ice reflects sunlight, which helps keep Earth's heat and energy in balance.

The only surface with a higher albedo than sea ice is snow. When snow is on top of thick sea ice, it can reflect up to 90 percent of the solar energy that reaches Earth. In the summer, the snow slows down the melting process. Once the snow begins to melt, it creates melt ponds, or pools of melted snow and ice. As these ponds grow bigger and deeper, the snow's albedo drops and the water warms.

A polar bear stands on a snow-covered iceberg in the Frozen Strait in Nunavut, Canada.

STEM Spotlight

Arctic sea ice is very important for a polar bear's survival. Polar bears use sea ice for traveling, hunting, resting, mating, and making dens. Polar bears spend half of their time hunting. They hunt in the winter months and store their energy during the summer months. Since sea ice is melting sooner in the spring and freezing later in the fall, polar bears have less time to hunt and must work harder to find food. They may not get the amount of food they need.

Chapter 3

CONSEQUENCES OF ARCTIC ICE LOSS

When Arctic sea ice melts faster than it can be replaced, less sunlight is reflected and Earth's temperature rises. Rising temperatures cause glaciers to melt. The bigger and deeper glaciers melt the fastest. This is a big problem in Greenland, one of the only two ice sheets on Earth.

Warmer temperatures in the summer months cause meltwater (water formed by melted snow and ice) to form on the surface of Greenland's glaciers. Meltwater flows down the side of the glacier and into fjords, narrow bodies of water that lead to the Arctic Ocean. Salty water from fjords beneath the glaciers cut or melt the glacier underneath, causing the glacier to break apart. As these glaciers break apart and melt, the ice sheet shrinks and water moves to the Arctic Ocean.

AN AERIAL VIEW OF GREENLAND

As Earth's climate changes, the amount of meltwater increases. More of Greenland's glaciers will break apart and melt. The melting of these glaciers causes sea levels to rise.

A slab of ice breaks apart from an iceberg in Disko Bugt on Greenland's western coast.

Rising Sea Levels and Coastal Communities

When sea levels rise, coastal communities are at risk. Roads, bridges, and tunnels are more open to flooding. When travel routes are closed to a city, it is difficult to get people the resources they need. Extreme storm events, such as hurricanes, happen more often due to rising sea levels and climate change. This causes even more danger to those living by or near the coast.

FLOODING ON THE STREETS OF PENNSYLVANIA FOLLOWING HURRICANE IDA

Food Production Problems

Unpredictable weather as a result of climate change affects food production. Heat waves, droughts, and flooding all cause damage to plants, making crops less available and more expensive. Climate change can also affect the way plants grow, making some foods less nutritious for humans and animals. In areas of the world where food is already difficult to get, climate change can make it even harder to get people the food they need to survive.

21

Wildlife Migration

Animals such as polar bears, walruses, and reindeer live in the Arctic and depend on sea ice to survive. These animals and many others have to adapt when less ice is in their surroundings. Sometimes they migrate closer to humans in Arctic communities. There, they find new dangers. The migration of these animals also affects the other animals that depend on them.

The Arctic is home to many animals, including reindeer.

STEM Spotlight

Loss of Arctic ice is a threat to Inuit communities. Inuit communities live in the Arctic and rely on sea ice to travel, hunt, and receive health care. The warming climate causes plants and animals to change locations. This makes finding food challenging. Thinning ice also makes it difficult and dangerous to hunt and fish. And stronger storms and larger waves as a result of climate change erode the coast where many Inuit communities live.

Chapter 4

STRATEGIES FOR ARCTIC ICE GROWTH

Global climate change is caused by high emissions of carbon dioxide and other greenhouse gases that get caught in a layer of Earth's atmosphere. When humans burn too many fossil fuels like coal, oil, and gas to create energy, greenhouse gases go into our atmosphere and trap heat. These gases act like a blanket that surrounds Earth and cause it to warm. Once these gases are used, they can't be reused.

One way to prevent global warming and Arctic ice loss is to reduce the use of fossil fuels. People are looking for more ways to get renewable energy. Renewable energy comes from natural resources that will always be there. For example, the sun will always shine, and wind will always blow.

Greenhouse gases trapped in the atmosphere cause Earth to warm.

Renewable Energy Sources

Clean energy strategies have reduced our use of fossil fuels. Many renewable sources are available to create energy.

People use sunlight for solar energy. Wind turbines turn wind into energy. Geothermal energy is made from heat from Earth's core. And the power of gravity from

SOLAR PANELS ON A HOUSE IN
THE NETHERLANDS

the moon is used to make tidal and wave energy. This strategy is being studied and may be helpful in the future. The more renewable energy is used, the less greenhouse gases will be released.

Pushing for Change

Many scientists, government leaders, and environmental activists are working on climate change solutions.

Wind turbines turn wind energy into electricity.

Arctic Angels is a youth-led group of young women from around the world who work on protecting the Arctic and Antarctica. They also participate in other environmental campaigns. Arctic Angels speak with members of their communities about climate change. They also press the importance of climate change to leaders that make policies to protect communities.

We need to prevent further climate change and keep the Arctic ice as thick and strong as we can. This will help protect all the living things on Earth.

Many people and groups such as researchers of the Arctic Ice Project (*shown here*) are looking for ways to protect the Arctic.

You Can Help!

We all can participate in Arctic ice loss solutions by being careful about the way we use energy. Here are things you, your friends, and your family members can do every day to save energy and fight climate change:

- Use energy-efficient light bulbs to save power and heat.
- Turn off lights and electronics when you're not using them.
- Recycle items to reduce waste and reuse products.
- Plant trees to help remove carbon dioxide from the air.
- Eat food before it goes bad to help lower food waste.
- Write to government leaders to urge them to take action against climate change.

Glossary

absorb: to take in and hold

climate change: a change in the usual weather conditions of a place over a long period

erode: to wear away Earth's surface by wind or water

floe: a separate patch of floating ice

fossil fuel: a fuel containing carbon that is formed from prehistoric animal and plant remains

glacier: a thick mass of ice on land that has built up from many seasons of snowfall

greenhouse gas: a gas in Earth's atmosphere that traps heat from the sun

Inuit: a group of Indigenous peoples of parts of Alaska, northern Canada, and Greenland

migrate: when an animal moves from one region to another

reflect: to throw back from the surface

Learn More

Bergin, Raymond. *Melting Ice*. Minneapolis: Bearport, 2022.

Furgang, Kathy. *Climate Change and Our Earth*. New York: PowerKids, 2022.

Kurtz, Kevin. *Climate Change and Rising Sea Levels*. Minneapolis: Lerner Publications, 2019.

NASA Climate Kids
https://climatekids.nasa.gov

National Geographic Kids: Polar Bear
https://kids.nationalgeographic.com/animals/mammals/facts/polar
-bear

Sea Ice Facts for Kids
https://kids.kiddle.co/Sea_ice

Index

Photo Acknowledgments

Image credits: Chase Dekker Wild-Life Images/Getty Images, p. 5; National Science Foundation, p. 6; kojoku/Shutterstock.com, p. 7; posteriori/Getty Images, p. 8; ljubaphoto/Getty Images, p. 11; Katvic/Shutterstock.com, p. 12; Paul Souders/Getty Images, p. 14; aroundtheworld.photography/Getty Images, p. 17; Paul Souders/Getty Images, p. 18; © Michael Stokes (CC by 2.0), p. 20; USDA Photo, p. 21; Melola/Shutterstock.com, p. 22; NASA, p. 25; Leoniek Van Der Vliet / EyeEm/Getty Images, p. 26; Ashley Cooper/Getty Images, p. 27; © Arctic Ice Project, p. 28.

Cover image: Paul Souders/Getty Images.